MY ROAD TO RECOVERY

Back And Forth *Over And Over*

Bill Graybeal

authorHOUSE®

AuthorHouse™
1663 Liberty Drive
Bloomington, IN 47403
www.authorhouse.com
Phone: 1-800-839-8640

Published by AuthorHouse 12/3/2012

ISBN: 978-1-4772-9524-3 (sc)
ISBN: 978-1-4772-9523-6 (e)

Library of Congress Control Number: 2012922583

Forward

On May 13, 2006 I had a massive heart attack in the emergency room of the local hospital. The doctors shocked me sixteen times to get my heart started. I was not serving the Lord and was bound in a porn and sex addiction. The addiction had my life in a mess. I was in bad financial condition because of the money I was spending on the addictions.

I was in intensive care in a coma on life support. They told my family to expect me to be in a vegetative state if I woke up. In reality they had no expectations that I would live. Around the 16th day of the coma they came and told my family it was time to give up and take me off of it. My family would not agree they were believing for a miracle. According to my wife within the next few days I started moving and opened my eyes slightly. She told the doctors this when they came in to check on me. She said they gave me a few commands to see how I would respond. I was told I responded to everything .

A day or so later I woke up to my wife asking me if I knew who she was. I am thinking why are you asking me that? Of course, I know who you are. So much for the vegetative state they were expecting.

It has been six years, and I am still recovering things I lost because of it. My brain was not getting proper oxygen during the coma, so I have brain damage in the area of memory and concentration.

This made it, so I had to retire and go on disability. According to the doctors' evaluation, I am considered to have a greater than 70% mental disability.

This book talks about the physical part of my recovery. It shows how I used the power of positive thinking saying and then doing to overcome the difficulties I was facing. I was raised in a positive encouraging Christian home. My parents made sure I was raised in church. They made sure I was taught the Word, whether I liked it or not. In spite of the environment, I was raised in I had a negative attitude about myself. They never gave up on feeding me positive and encouraging words. This book shows how I quit using the negative attitudes.

The idea behind this book came from all the back and forth over and over, I had to do during recovery. The devil tried so hard to use it against me. I will show you how I used it for my good to make me stronger in all areas of my life as time went on.

I have a lot of fun when I write. This book was a lot more fun than the others because it is more about the physical part of recovery. It was written when I was going through the hard times it talks about. I thought it would be a lot more fun to write about how much fun I was having instead of how strenuous it was at the time.

My parents raised me to become a minister. Instead I became a sex and porn addict. It looks like all of that praying did not work. Read my books and tell me if you still think I did not become what they prayed I would.

At the time of the heart attack they put a pacemaker in. They last about six years so recently I had to get a new one. When I went in to talk to the Dr. about what to expect I met the doctor who was there when I had the heart attack. About a third of the appointment was spent telling me what to expect the next day. The other two-thirds he was telling me how lucky I was. He told me that only ten percent of the people that have a heart attack as bad as mine survive. Of that a small percentage are not in a vegetative state of mind.

I know my parents prayers saved my life. I can remember my momma looking at me square in the face and telling me I would not go to hell because she was putting prayers in place to prevent it. I am not lucky. I had a praying momma.

Another thing I heard often after the heart attack was God is not through with you yet. I know this is true, and I am going to show you that in spite of everything I am going to take back everything and will become everything the Lord originally intended for my life. I don't care how hard it is. In my book that is what makes it so much fun.

ACKNOWLEDGEMENTS

I could not resist giving the devil credit for helping me recover. His big mouth has given me the drive I needed. I enjoyed him telling me the reasons I was not getting anywhere. A wanta bet watch me attitude was my best friend during these times.

I want to thank my parents and all the wonderful ladies who taught me the things of God. When I was young, I was called a momma's boy because I ran to momma when I was in trouble. That hurt at the time and I spent a lot of time crying because of it. When I was running to her she was teaching me the attitudes I write about in my books. Now when people call me a momma's boy I say; "I sure am and I am proud of it."

When mom died, I was eighteen. The Lord brought other ladies who took her place as my teachers. My step aunt, her mom and my step mom are all people that I have to thank. If it was not for them and what they taught me I would not be able to write the things I do. Thank you.

I had a wonderful dad also. I have to thank him for the great work ethic I have. The proudest times of my life have been when people tell me I am a hard worker. I heard that said to my dad all the time. When people say that about me, I think to myself I do it like dad did it.

I thank God for my Christian home all the time.

TABLE OF CONTENTS

BACK AND FORTH

I was told the way I was going to recover my memory was by doing things over and over until I could remember. Exercise was needed to regain my strength. Not a really easy thing to do after you have been through a heart attack. This is the light-hearted way I dealt with it.

In the early stages of recovery, when I was sitting in my room I would think I need something in the other room. Most of the time I forgot when I got there. Back to my room I would go. After sitting there for a while I would remember what I needed. So back I would go only to forget again. The enemy would say; "See how damaged your mind is." I would say: "Don't you see what is going on? The more I go back and forth the stronger I get."

I was gaining physical and mental strength because the way you get it back is by doing things over and over again. After you have done it enough it gets easier to remember like you are supposed to. They told me as I exercised physically my concentration and memory would get stronger. I would have to add a very long time. So sitting there feeling sorry for myself would not help me recover.

You have short-term memory and long-term memory. A good example of short-term memory is taking my shoes or watch off and putting them down somewhere for the night. In the morning, I could never remember where I put them. Why didn't I put them in the same place every night like they told me? I tried that but the next morning I could never remember where the same place was. There were too many same places to remember. There was the same place for my clothes. The same place for the food in the refrigerator. The same place for my Bible, my IPod, the remote, the movie I wanted to watch. The same places were endless.

I could never find scriptures I was trying to stand on in the Bible. Is the book I am looking for in the New Testament or Old? The only books I could remember were the first three books of the Old Testament and the first four of the New Testament. Then, there was the problem of finding the verse. Why didn't I make it easy on myself and use a concordance? There were several reasons. How is the word spelled? I had a hard time remembering how to spell my own name in the beginning. I sure was not going to remember how to spell a word. Another reason I did not use a concordance was because I could not remember the order of the letters in the alphabet. Then when I found what I was looking for I would forget where it told me to look. As soon as I looked away I forgot. It was back and forth between the concordance and the Bible over and over again.

The frustration brought me to a point where I began to understand something. I was raised in a Christian home, and I have heard the Word all my life. It is already in me all I need to do is use it, and it will work.

The devil often challenged me on verses I was standing on. He would sometimes ask where it is in the Bible? I would always answer; "I don't know, but I know it is and you do to." You will never beat the devil if you do not learn to stand up and talk back to him. Tell him you know the Word, and will show him any time he wants to try you.

I would go into the store and go to an isle to get an item. By the time I got there, I forgot the reason I was in that isle. No big thing was my thinking; I will move on to the next item in my list. I would never remember the first item until I was on the other side of the store. So back I would go only to forget again. This would go on and on sometimes. The devil would try to remind me how messed up my memory was. I would say; "It is great exercise don't you think? What did they tell me in rehab? Back and forth over and over is how you get stronger and recover the things you have lost. I don't know about you I'm having fun."

I was so weak I could hardly stand up. I can remember one time I was in a store waiting to check out, and you will never guess what the lady ahead of me was doing. She was paying for her purchase in pennies. At first, I thought help God; I cannot stand that long. The Lord said look at it this way, the longer you stand the stronger you get. Not only do you get stronger physically you get stronger in patience. That is the way I started looking at it. Longer just means stronger.

I will not give up or give in on the plans; I know the Lord has for my life. I will not give in to the limitations of mental handicaps. I have heart disease, and I am pre-diabetic. My attitude has always been I may have these limitations, but they do not have me. I am not worried or stressed about the things I have to do to keep things under control. I am not going to sit here dealing with all the pressure these things could bring. How you handle the pressure depends upon your attitude towards it. I know it is going to make me stronger and better prepared to recover all I need to. I am not worried I am having fun.

I Am Not Going To
Lose This Time

I lost so many things because I gave in to the devil and what he said about me. Most of all I lost the joy I would have had if would have done things right. Be careful how you look at your past. Do not let it make you feel bad about yourself. When you do you are opening the door so he can defeat you again.

"I wish I would have listened to all the encouraging words I was taught. If I would have listened, I coulda and woulda done all the wonderful things the Lord purposed me to do." I will not let what I coulda and shoulda done stop me from taking back the ministry the devil stole from me. I will do what I have to no matter how hard it is, or how long it takes. Back and forth over and over until I get it right I do not care. I won't lose this time.

The devil tried to make the heart attack have a disabling effect in my life. The Lord could use it as a set-up for my come-back because of my attitude. To make it a set-up required my participation or it would not work. I had to have the attitude and use the words and actions that would make it a come-back. You have to do the things that are going to get you in a position and condition so the Lord can use it as a come-back.

You have to learn to use what the devil uses against you. He was continuously, persistently putting things in my way to try to get me to quit. My attitude was if it is continuously, and persistently you want that is the way it will be. His constant persistent developed that kind of attitude in me. Constantly, and persistently I showed the devil I could, and I would. The pressure of his constant, persistence against my constant persistence is why my constant persistence is so strong. Always do your best persistently and there is no way the devil can beat you. Believe me, he is going to try as hard as he can. That is going to make you the strong person you were purposed to be.

How do I know I will reach my goals this time? I always failed in the past. Why wouldn't I lose this time as well? The difference is I won't quit like I always did. Quitters never win losers never quit no matter what. I coulda and shoulda and sure wish I woulda. That is what drives me to become what I coulda and shoulda been.

BE BOLD AND AGGRESSIVE

A bold aggressive attitude is the only kind of attitude the devil is going to understand. He will not back off until you make him. An aggressive attitude means attacking and invading. It is assertive and forceful. Assertive means a confident self-assured decisive attitude. An attitude that knows what it is after and will not give up until it is in possession.

We have to invade the areas of our life that the devil has taken and forcibly remove him. To invade means to go after forcefully and take possession of. The Lord gave the children of Israel the promise land. The possession did not come until they went in and took what the Lord promised them. Until they did they went around in the circle of doubt fear and defeat. That is the way it will be until you get a bold, aggressive and forceful attitude. Trust me, I know I have been there and done that most of my life.

I thought I would fail so most of the time I would not show up and try to overcome my fears. How in the world are you going to win the battle if you do not show up? Since the heart attack, I have made it a point to show up with an aggressive bold attitude. Sometimes all I would say was; "Devil I am still here." It is impossible for him to beat you when you never give up.

The most important thing in recovery of any kind is to show up and do the things you must to recover like you are supposed to. If you do not show up and do the work, you are not going anywhere.

I never realized my dreams because I did not have a bold aggressive attitude. I had a timid passive attitude when it seemed too hard. My attitude was if I make it ok, but if I do not I guess that was not the Lord's plan for my life.

The only way you make it is by being aggressively determined and relentlessly persistent. The answer is not in being passive and defensive all the time. You have to have an attitude that says I am going after it and there is nothing in this world or hell that will stop me. Do not forget to include the devil. You have to invade the enemies' ground.

Be assertive, positive and confident in the abilities the Lord put in you. Insist upon your rights through the power of the Holy spirit that is in you. You have to claim your rights as a child of God with confidence and force (Luke 10:19).

You will see as you read on that I was never passive, shy or timid about taking back my health. I did not make my goal every day, but I promise myself I would go one step farther than I did yesterday.

Everything

I will take back everything the devil robbed from me. He took everything from me. Why would I settle for anything less? The devils' plan is to leave you defeated. He wants you to feel like you are nothing more than a worthless nobody.

I lost when I left Bible college at the age of eighteen. That was the beginning of years of losing everything. I lost cars, a house, nearly my family and nearly my life. I am not going to back off now that I understand who I am and what I am.

I lost the car and house because I feared a neighbor that I thought was threatening me. I ran to another state to get away from the situation. I was not working so I was unable to make the car and house payments. When I bought that house, I paid 53,000 dollars twenty years ago. Today that house is worth about $250,000. I wish I would not have let the enemy steal it. What a great position I would be in today.

I could let that bother me. I drive past that house occasionally. I tell the devil as I pass he is going to pay for what I allowed him to do. Too often we let failures stop us when we should be using them to drive us. I made that mistake before I won't make it again should be our attitude. Do not look at failure as anything other than experience that will get you to where the Lord is taking you. I often say, "Devil you do not seem to understand I have been there and done that. I am to experienced to allow you to get me in that position again."

I know what I was purposed to be. I have been told all my life. The only one that did not believe it was me. The only thing I have done to become it was to start believing it. Now that I believe it, I will become it and nothing will stop me.

The devil has tried many times. Maybe that day I did not make it to the goal I set for myself. He tried to get me to look at it as a defeat. As far as I was concerned it was not. I was not strong enough to make it yet. Do not be defeated by levels of recovery that you are not strong enough to take possession of yet. Patient persistence will always get you in the condition so you can take possession.

Because of the damage, the heart attack did to my memory and concentration it is very hard for me to put things I write about into the spoken word. I have had people say to me you cannot speak it, but you can write it is the way you should think. I am thinking that would not be everything. Everything would be being able to get up and minister it through the spoken Word. That is the Lord's original purpose in my life that is what I am going after.

I learned the hard way that the life you give in to is the life you live in. I want to live in the life the Lord originally intended. The Lord's original purpose for your life was His final decision. All you have to do is make it your final decision and not settle for anything less.

The devil constantly tries to get me to believe that writing is the only purpose the Lord has for my life. His original intention for me was to go to Bible School and become a minister. That desire is still in me. Even though I did not make it in Bible School the things the Lord has taken me through have taught me a lot of things I would not have learned in Bible School. It may take me several years before I recover sufficiently to speak it well enough to put into spoken words. As far as I am concerned that is the everything I am going after. "I will take back everything you have stolen devil. Go ahead try my attitude. I hope you do. What part of everything do you not understand?"

Every Where The Soles Of You Feet Shall Tread

This verses is found in Deuteronomy 11:24. It is a promise given to the children of Israel concerning the promise land. It is a promise that we can use in our Christian walk. I use it daily in my recovery.

For several months I felt like I was going to fall if I got very far from something stable to hold on to. I decided that I would always get up and go where I needed to and nothing would stop me. I may have to sit down and rest a lot. That will not stop me from getting there.

This verse tells me everywhere the soles of my feet tread shall be mine. The only way that will happen is for me to get up and put my faith into action. The verses says everywhere so I am not going to fear going everywhere. There were days at first when with every step I said, "mine." I told the devil that in spite of how I felt I would walk everywhere and I would not fall down. I never fell down once during recovery. To show you what a miracle that is you have to understand I live in Alaska where there is snow and ice on the side walks six months of the year. Not to slip and fall at least once during the year when you are normal is somewhat of a miracle.

Everywhere I walked at first was pretty close to home. As I was persistent everywhere got farther. One thing I really enjoyed was the devil telling me to use one of those motorized carts in stores.

Sometimes it would be so hard not to give in. There were two reasons I refused. Number one my mind and concentration were so messed up I would probably run over someone. The other was I promised myself that I would walk everywhere no matter what.

When I was in the hospital they had me walking daily a short time after I came out of the coma. They do not let you lay there and do nothing. The way you get your heart stronger is by exercising it. So when I was refusing the motorized cart I was not doing anything that would harm me. I was in fact doing something that was going to make me stronger as time went on.

I have a disabled card in my car that allows me to park close to the building. In the early stages of recovery it was a blessing. As I began to get stronger I enjoyed parking farther from the building so I would get the exercise I needed. Most of the time I was still very weak, that did not stop me. The Word says everywhere I put the soles of my feet so I am going to put the soles of my feet everywhere I can so I recover like I should.

Of course it was hard I started walking just as few days after I almost died. It stays hard if you do not take action and do what you are told so it will become easier as time goes on. Cardiac recovery is getting on a treadmill for 20 minutes and then a stationary bike for 20 minutes. It was the hardest thing I have ever done. At the beginning I just barely did 10 minutes at the slowest possible pace. At the end I was going at the pace they asked me to with a lot more ease. In this book you will hear me talk a lot about exercise because that is the way you rehabilitate your heart.

Not only will exercise make you feel better it will make you do better. My life is better than it has ever been. It is because I do things that make it better. I believe in myself and in what the Lord says about me.

I plant my feet solidly on the Word and I take back everywhere the soles of my feet tread. Everywhere and everything the Lord promised me is mine and I am going to take it so, "deal with it devil."

If God Be For You

Probably, the biggest lesson I learned during recovery is if God be for you, you have to be for you also. If you are not the Lord cannot do the things He purposed in your life. The only one powerful enough to stop you is you.

It would have been easy to stay in bed. On top of feeling lousy and weak they had me on nine medications. If you have not been on that many mediations at once you do not know how hard it is. Not only do you have to fight feeling lousy because of what happened to you, you also have to fight the effects of the medication. It is not easy, and it is not fun. It took me almost two years before the medication did not affect me.

Always understand God is for you. He is always there to help you. He is a very present help in time of trouble. However, you have to have the correct attitudes and use the correct words to overcome the difficulties you are facing.

If your thinking and saying is against you, there is nothing the Lord can do for you. Until you understand the power your thinking and saying has in your life you will not be in a position for the Lord to help you. I promised the devil and myself that not one negative word would cross my lips no matter how difficult it was. That was the very first thing I put in position because I knew how important it was.

My primary exercise was walking because it was something I enjoy doing. I always said, "If I feel lousy so what? I will walk farther today. No pain, no gain, therefore, I will gain despite the pain." Every time I went on a walk, I set a goal. Today's walk was always farther than yesterdays. Sometimes it was just a few steps farther and sometimes it was a lot farther.

The devil and his big mouth was such a encouragement. He would always try to get me down because of the short distances I would go at first. He would say; "you are proud of yourself for walking up to the end of the block and back? That's not very far." I would always point out what it was the week before. "Last week I could only walk around the house, and you are telling me to the end of the block is not very far? Next week, it will be around the block. If I were you, I would shut up you are the one that is driving me so hard." Don't let the difficulty of recovery stop you let it drive you.

The tough is in the rough. The rough the Lord allows you to go through will make you the strong person He purposed you to be. I can remember crying at the beginning thinking Lord how will I make it through this. He said, "Through this, I am going to show you how tough you really are. You have always been weak and very easy to defeat. I am going to use this to make you the person you were purposed to be. When this is over you are going to be a person that is impossible to defeat. It will be impossible because you will never give up."

I know the Lord is for me, and I know the devil is going to be against me. As far as I am concerned, I am not worried about who is against me. The Lord and I are a majority so what do I have to worry about?

Where your confidence is there will you be also. You can do what the Lord says you can unless you think you can't. Having no confidence in yourself is having no faith in the gifts the Lord put in you. I have had many wonderful gifts in me all my life. I never lived in them because I never had confidence in myself. The devil did not stop me; he does not have that power, unless I give it to him. Lack of confidence in myself and the gifts that are in me stopped me. The most important person that needed to be for me was not. The person that stopped me was me.

My writing is not about the harm my past has done to me. It is about the experience I gained. Recently, I was told by a doctor that I was one of the toughest people he ever met. I wanted to tell him do you know how I got so tough? I have taken all the rough and used it to become tough. You will not become tough if you give up or give in when it gets rough. The tough comes when you stay firm and unyielding in attitude when it is rough. I could have learned many of these things a long time ago. I never became tough because I never stayed when it was rough. This time I used the pain of going through the difficulty of recovery for my gain. I have been taught so much by this long recovery concerning what I am in God's plans in my life. The things I have gained from this experience are worth it.

God was for me and my parents were, but I was not. It does not matter who is for you if you are not the devil will beat you every time. If God be for me, and I be for me, there is nothing in the world or hell that can stop me. I have to be persistent and patient as the Lord prepares me and positions me for the plans He has for me.

Like the children of Israel, I went around and around in the wilderness of doubt and fear before I came to the place that I would finally face and overcome my doubts and fears. I have entered into the Lords promise and purpose because I have taken what is rightfully mine.

God is for me, and I am going to show everybody what they can do if they are for themselves. You are the only one that can keep you from your dreams. If you think and say you will never make it, you never will. You do not have the right attitude. The altitude you go in God's plans for you is determined by your attitude. Your condition in is always determined by your position. Do you take a positive position? Do you take your position in Christ Jesus and keep the devil in his position? Do you allow the devil to determine your position and therefore, your condition?

One Step Farther
Than Yesterday

This is an attitude I started using in the early stages of recovery. I would never end a walk, unless I went one step farther than I did yesterday. As long as I keep taking one extra step I am gaining ground. It is not very much, but it is better than yesterday. One additional step a day means seven additional steps a week and thirty in a month. Eventually, I am going to reach my goal.

In the early months, I used telephone poles as goals. Often it would take me a week or more to get enough strength to make it to the pole. I made sure I went at least a few steps farther each day. When I finally made it to the pole, I did it over again with the next pole.

The important thing is not that you make it to your goal the first time it is that you stay persistent. You never succeed if you quit trying. You always succeed when you refuse to give up. Don't let the difficulty stop you use it to drive you. Sometimes you are only able to go one step further. So what! It is farther than you went yesterday.

You have to keep your eyes on the goal in spite of what you are going through to get there. Feeling lousy and very weak was the way I felt most of the time. It is not easy to exercise like they tell you to when you don't feel like it. You can sit there feeling sorry for yourself, but that is not going to get you anywhere.

At first, I prayed that the Lord would make me stronger, so I could do the things I used to. That did not make me stronger. Doing the exercises did. Of course, the Lord was with me helping me. I might add the devil was there also with his big mouth trying to get me to give in. Showing him I could and would was the fun part.

Don't let just barely making your goal defeat you. When you have worked hard to reach your goal, and it is just barely you are winning not losing. The only way you lose is by quitting. You have come a long way from not being able to make it at all. Use how far you have come as encouragement to drive you to keep going. The devil wants you to look at how far you have to go. I always turned that around and said, "Yeah but look how far I have come."

Just barely comes before being able to do it without effort. And most of the time it is after just barely making it for a long time. The important thing is do not give up or give in when it is just barely.

When I started writing my first book, I could just barely sit in the chair and type for any length of time. It took a lot of persistence and patience only writing a few lines. With a lot of persistence, it later became a few paragraphs. After a while, it became a few chapters. Now I am writing a few books at a time. If I would have given up when I was only able to do things just barely I would not be in the position I am today.

That first book is published because I had the right attitudes when I could just barely write. It is full of chapters written when I could just barely figure things out. I was just barely able to put it together so it could be published. When I sent it to the publisher, I told the Lord it is so messed up because of the way it is put together. He told me if people are looking at the mess they will not get the message. If they are listening to the message, they will not notice the mess, and the mess will not matter to them. If you are in a mess, and your eyes are on the mess you will not get the message, if your eyes are on the message, you will not let the mess bother you.

Don't quit when it gets hard. Hard does not become easy without constant persistence. I have mental handicaps that do not stop me from writing because I know that is what the Lord purposed. I will never get to the point where it is easy if I do not constantly challenge the handicaps. I do not allow them to stop me; I use them to drive me to become better at what I know the Lord purposed me to do.

The Message In The Mess

The mess I was in at the time of the heart attack was bad. I was so financially messed up that I am still working that out. On top of that I had medical bills to deal that were astronomical. I was a porn and sex addict and I was about to lose my wife. The Lord had so many messages for me in the mess that I was in.

I learned I needed to start standing up for myself and believing in myself. If you don't believe in yourself, you can never be the person the Lord purposed you to be. The heart attack put me in a position where I started believing all the Word that was in me. It helped me to start saying positive things about myself and the things I could do. I never talked about the difficulties I was going through. If you do that you will never get through. Words have power that can take you through any difficulty. They have the power of the attitude that is behind them. Be very careful what you say about yourself. It will be your reality.

I stopped letting the power of my negative words work against me. The Word says in Romans 8:31 "If God be for us who can be against us. The only person that has the power to take the power out of that scripture is you. If God be for you and your words are against you your words are going to win. Why wouldn't they? You believe what you are thinking and saying more than the Word.

The heart attack had a positive effect in my life because it changed my attitude. I always gave up on things I knew the Lord had for me to do before it happened. After it my attitude changed to, "You knocked me down devil, but you did not knock me out. I am still here and everything I have allowed for you to steal from me; I am going to take back."

Recovery has taught me that you don't get back strength unless you persistently do the things that allow you to take it back. So it is with the ministry I lost because of doubts and fears. I do not get that back unless I do the things I must to take it back.

I knew because of the way I was raised that the reason I did not die was because the Lord was not through with me yet. The purpose the Lord has for you is not over until He says it is. He knows what is in you, and He has plans for your life, and nothing can stop it except you.

The heart attack in the natural was a major set-back. I was not able to work because of what happened to me mentally. I was taught that when the Lord closes a door, he always opens a better one. The new door was going to allow me to write without any concern for holding down a job.

At the time, I was really believing I would go back to work. My reasoning was wouldn't it be a miracle after all that happened? It would have been, however, the Lord had different plans. A lot of the time the Lord chooses to take us through the difficulties instead of taking us out of them. The message the Lord wants to get across to us are in the difficulties He is taking us through.

The Lord put things in position as far back as twenty years ago that put me in the position I am today. In the late seventies, I was working for the school district in Point Barrow, Alaska. I only worked there for about three years before I had to quit because my oldest son was born. The job was working in a children's home taking care of troubled kids of all ages. With two kids of our own my wife and I decided we had to quit.

For the next 15 years or so I worked for myself without any type of medical coverage and without any retirement. Not a smart move

I understand now because of the position it could have put me in at the time of the heart attack. The Lord knew the position I was going to be in today twenty years ago though.

After working for myself for so long, I decided I needed to get a regular job with benefits. The only place I could find that would hire me was the school district here in Fairbanks, Alaska. At the time, I did not understand that this was part of the set-up the Lord was putting in place for what I am doing today. I later found out that the union I was in twenty years earlier is the same union I had to join when I started working for the school district here. They had to grandfather me in under the union agreement that was in place twenty years ago. Under that agreement, I do not pay anything for all the medication I have to take. I pay very little for the medical things I have to have done. I do not have to worry about the position I am in today because the Lord had it planned out all along.

The Lord even set-up how I was going to make it financially after I had to quit my job. I applied for Social Security, and they said it would take months if not years. The Lord had other plans. The month after my regular job stopped paying Social Security started. I am told often that I am lucky because things worked out so well. That is not luck my friend. That is God taking care of one of his own.

Tell me if this sounds like luck. On May 13, 2006, I was at home and started having chest pains. I thought they were pains caused by the problems I was having in my stomach. I decided I should go to the emergency room to have them checked out. I drove to the emergency room and started to check in. In the emergency room I fell down on the floor dead. They shocked me 16 times and worked for an hour before I was somewhat stabilized. Was having the heart attack in the emergency-room luck or special delivery. If it would have happened anywhere else I would not have survived. The doctor told me later that he did not understand why he shocked me 16 times. He told me that was a lot more than the norm. Was I lucky he did or was the hand of God guiding him?

The mess showed me how the Lord was always there in spite of the way I was living. Preparing me and positioning me for what I am doing today. It showed me that I have always had the right words and attitudes in me. You can be taught all the correct attitudes all of your life like I was and live a defeated life like I did. You will never act in God's plans for your life until you start acting on the things that are going to get you in that condition and position.

The message I have in my heart I learned in the many messes the Lord took me through to get me in the position I am today. After the heart attack I was never worried about the mess I was in. I was not looking at the mess I was looking at the message in it.

Under no circumstances do you ever give up or give in or that is where you will live under the circumstances. Keep going one step farther today and you cannot be beat. Don't get discouraged when you don't make your goal the first time. Use the failure to drive you not stop you. How tough you are when it is rough determines how the rough effects you. It also determines how long you stay in the rough. If you allow it the rough will make you act in a negative way. Don't allow it to have that affect on you. Allow the challenge to make you the tough person you were purposed to be.

This month has been a real mess for my wife and I. I went to the doctor and they found a blood clot in my heart. In order for them to deal with it I had to stay in the ICU. Now days they have all kinds of ways that they can look inside your heart and see what they need to do. The blood clot was removed by taking a medication for a year. I had to stay in the ICU though for a week until my blot clot factor was where they wanted it. I saw how powerful a positive encouraging attitude is. My nurses said I was an easy patient to deal with. My attitude was if I can minister to them, by the way, I think say and do that is what I will do. I never threw my religion at them; I just lived it. Actions speak louder than words anyway don't they? "I was having fun weren't you devil? He he Gotcha!"

I Am Not Strong
Enough Yet

I made up what I call the attitude of yet. The things that I used to do I could not do again right away. Most things took a long time to recover. I am telling you from experience that when you have to work hard for so long to regain the ability to do things, it can get very stressful. Not worrying or being anxious about the things I was not strong enough to do yet made it fun as far as I am concerned.

My car sat in my yard for over a year. My memory and concentration were so bad that it looked like it would be impossible to get behind the wheel again. My attitude when I would look at my car was I am not in the position and condition, so I can drive you YET. I fed on the fact that with persistence and patience I would be in the condition to be able to. I never once went out and tried to drive until the Lord told me now is the time to try. I always heard the Lord tell me not yet, it is not time to try yet. The day came when I heard the Lord say, "ok now." Now you have healed to the point where you are in the position and condition to be successful.

Sometimes we get discouraged that we cannot do the things the Lord promised yet. We must understand that there has to be persistence and a whole lot of patience as we recover to the point where we are in condition, so we can take possession of that which the Lord promised. Don't get discouraged by the fact that God has not done the things He promised yet. He does not have you in the position and condition, so he can use you like He wants to yet.

You might be saying I have prayed for my loved ones for so long, and it does not seem like it is working. If the Lord let you see the preparation and positioning He is doing in that loved one's life you would see how wonderful His plans are. Don't get discouraged bc encouraged by the fact that the Lord is positioning things in their life. After He has done that they will be in a position to accept the Lord.

There are a lot of thing in my life and recovery that have not happened YET. All I have to say is it is not time YET. When the time comes you will see those things come to pass. And I might add nothing in hell will stop that. "Get it devil."

After the heart attack I had people come to me and ask me to give my testimony. The Lord always said, "not YET." At the time, I did not fully understand. "Why won't you let me give my testimony YET Lord?" One of the reasons was that the Lord did not have in me what He wanted to put in me YET. Another reason was I was not in the condition and position mentally and spiritually to be successful YET. To try and operate at a level you are not capable of yet always results in failure. Wait until you are strong enough to operate at that level with ease, and you will be successful. You have to do the work that is needed to be able to maintain your strength at each new level.

Getting stressed and worried is not going to get you anywhere. Calm persistence is the thing that will get you into position for each new level. It can get very hard and stressful at times that is why you have to stay calm as you go through the process of recovery.

Why worry or stress when you are facing a battle that you know you are going to win? I cannot see where that is any fun. I do not see how it is going to get you anywhere.

Nehemiah 8: 10 says, " The Joy of the Lord is my strength." That is how I choose to handle it. Why stress when you can have fun regaining things, you lost? All I have been through was just a set-up to position me and prepare me for what the Lord has for me. What could be more exciting than that?

There is always a time when the Lord will tell you not now. With persistence and patience there will always come a time when He says; "ok now." Getting worried about the Lord's timing does not help. Being patient as He prepares and positions things is the only way to go. It makes it a lot more fun as well. That is what it is all about right?

Persistence And Patience

Persistence means to continue steadfastly and firmly in purpose and course of action in spite of opposition. To last and endure tenaciously and to be insistent in what you are going after.

To insist means to assert and maintain firmly. The definition I like is to demand and to persist in demanding. The devil is not going to give us any ground until we are demanding that he give back the ground he has taken. You do not get ground unless you take it by the force of insistent.

The word assert means to act with assurance, confidence and force. It means to act strongly and positively taking your place in Christ Jesus. The word assurance means to act full of confidence. To act in the assurance of the success the Lord promises in His Word. You will never succeed if you are not full of confidence that you can do what He says you can. Remember where your confidence is there will you be also.

In the past, I was always a shy timid person with no self-confidence or belief in my abilities. I never asserted myself in assurance and confidence in the purpose of being the minister that the Lord purposed. If there is no assertion and no assurance, there will be no success. Success is proceeded by an attitude full of confidence in your abilities. You have to be free from doubt and fear of not being successful. Certain that what you are going after you will possess. It means you will be right here, and still here until you obtain what the Lord promised.

In spite of what the devil has brought or will bring you will act in persistence and patience until you are in possession of the promise. The word spite means in disregard or defiance of. Acting in assurance and confidence in who you are and what you are in site of anything and everything the devil brings to defeat you. My favorite definition of spite is to thwart and annoy. "I love that definition don't you devil? What do you think? I don't really care what you think because I gotcha right where I wantcha."

Patience in the Biblical sense means waiting full of expectancy that the Lord will do what he promised when it is His time. His time a lot of the time depends how long it takes Him to get us into position and condition, so He can use us like He planned.

I have always told the devil, "You know I am not in that condition and position YET. Just wait my times coming and when my time comes your time has come."

God cannot use you until persistence, and patience has it's perfect work. They are what gets you in the position and condition for the Lord to use you. Until you are in the right position and condition, there will be no possession.

But I Don't Feel Like It

What does that have to do with it? Let me tell you that in recovery there are a lot of days you do not feel like it. If I would have acted on the way I felt I would have never made it. After the heart attack I felt like I was damaged in such a way that I could never recover. I have never felt weakness in all areas of my life like I did then. They were feelings that went on for months and months and some of the effects I still feel. I learned you never recover like you should if you act on how you feel. Feeling better is on the other side of doing what you have to, so you do.

You have to be patient it takes time to gain your strength back. I am as strong as I am today because I have six years of doing what I had to behind me. Let me tell you that has taken a lot of patient persistence. Many days of thinking, saying and showing the devil I was still here persisting in spite of how I felt.

You might be thinking you don't understand what I have been through. You don't understand how hard this is. I have learned the harder it is the better it is for you in the end. Do not run away from hard, go after it. In the end, it is going to make you the tough person the Lord wants you to be.

If you act on the way you feel you will not gain strength. You have to act on what is truth. And the truth is you get stronger with persistence and patience. If you want to keep feeling like you do don't do anything. If you want to feel better do whatever it takes no matter how hard it is, or how long it takes. Always listen to those who are trying to encourage you like the wonderful ladies who helped me in rehab. In the beginning, I wanted to slap them. Now I think they are wonderful ladies who really know what they are doing and have a gift for it.

How you recover and how long it takes is determined by your attitude and position on the subject. Your recovery will go nowhere if you do not get off your butt and go somewhere. That may be to the other end of the store over and over. You are not sitting on your butt doing nothing you are gaining strength by going back and forth. Under no circumstances let how you feel dictate what you will do to gain back your strength.

IT IS NOT ABOUT WHERE YOU ARE

It Does matter where you are you must always show the devil who you are. If you do not he will keep you right where you are. There is no way he is going to do that to me. My attitude is always I am right here, and I am still here. You can count on the fact that I will take back all the things I have lost.

When I woke up from the coma, it triggered all the things, the Lord and my parents put in me. My attitude was, "devil now you have made me mad. If you think, I do not know how to make it through this you have another think coming. I don't care where I am in recovery. I don't care how hard, or how long it takes I will only act on who I am no matter where I am." When I went back to the hospital recently the devil was saying, "ok let's see how you talk in this mess. You talk big and bold let's just see how you talk and act in the ICU." I never change my attitude. I was as positive in the ICU as I was when I was out of it. I had the attitude, "Devil nothing you can bring will change my attitude. You are dealing with someone who knows how to act no matter where he is." It has taken me most of my life to finally see who I am and what I am in God's plans for my life. And I will not act any other way I don't care where I am.

All my life I have had a why me attitude. "Lord you tell me I am supposed to be a very positive uplifting messenger of your Word. Why did you make me so shy and timid? Lord I just do not understand your plan. You say I am one thing. I feel like you made me a totally different kind of person."

I realize now even though I was negative the Lord was teaching me how to live a positive life. I can remember years and years of encouragement from my parents. It did not matter how negative I was they were always positive. I could not move those who were encouraging me out of being positive. I tried to talk them out of the positive attitudes they had with me many times. It never worked they were unmovable. I would always say; "Yeah but what if you are wrong." I see now that's the kind of attitude I had all the time. Now there is nothing you can do to talk me out of being positive.

The heart attack was something I brought on myself because I was not watching my cholesterol. It should have been a real set-back. It has forced me into the attitudes I was taught all my life. It has shown me I am what I was told I was, and I can do what I was told I could do.

I am what I am because my parents told me what the Lord's purpose for my life was, and they would not move. They saw the seed to feed, and that was the only seed they would feed. Nothing ever moved them from that attitude and position.

The heart attack that should have been a set-back has been a set-up. I made it through recovery like I have because of the seeds they fed in my life. They always said, You have to show the devil who and what you are no matter where you are. Now that I understand it is not hard to be that person.

I changed because what were always negative attitudes and positions are now positive attitudes and positions. I will always show the devil I have the same attitude when it seems like things are falling down around me as when everything is going great. "That's the way I am devil so deal with it. That is the way I was taught to be so that's the way I will be and there is nothing you can do about it."

I Have Limitations They Don't Have Me

Physically, and mentally I have a lot of limitations. Physically, I have to watch the way I eat because I am at a high risk of another heart attack if I do not watch my cholesterol. A blocked artery caused my heart attack. I am also pre-diabetic, which does not make it any easier.

I could have the attitude of, I know all the foods high in cholesterol are not good for me, but you just don't understand. I can't give them up. What will I do if I cannot drink soda and eat ice cream? ANSWER: live longer. What will happen if I do not give them up is the question? If I do not I will have another heart attack sooner or later. There are so many things I cannot eat. With the right education, there are so many things I can still eat. I need to eat a lot fish because of the omega three in it. I love fish. Where is the negative in that?

I still drink coffee and have soda. I drink it in moderation, and I drink diet caffeine free. I hear people say all the time, but you don't understand I cannot live without it. If you are not careful, you will put yourself in the position I am in. I learned the hard way that you cannot live with it if you have conditions that it will affect.

Be aware that the way you are eating and not exercising puts you in the position to have problems later. All my life I was very healthy.

I could count the times I went to the doctor on both hands. I ate anything I wanted. Little did I know that all that cholesterol I was eating was building up and in time would almost kill me. Now I am paying the consequences. I am handicapped because of the way I ate.

Limitations in what I can eat does not have me depressed and discouraged. I have changed the way I eat and am enjoying every minute of it. I am writing this in a fast-food restaurant. I am on a five-mile walk and wanted a coffee. And I wanted to sit down and write this before I forget. I am actually writing this on napkins because I have no paper. There are smells of cooking food and a menu of a lot of foods high in calories and cholesterol in front of me. Am I tempted to order something not good for me. It smells and looks so good. I am not in the least bit tempted. I have the way I eat under control and there is not one burger and fries or even a milkshake that will get me out of that attitude. I will not eat anything that is not good for me. I don't care how good it smells or looks.

I have sent food back because it does not fit the way I eat. In the ICU I sent back more than one meal because it did not fit into my diet. It sure did look good that baked potato and steak though. I know if I eat it, my sugar and my cholesterol will go way up. I could say but you don't understand it smells and looks so good. I don't want people coming to look at me in a casket because I would not eat right. That almost happened to me. I plan on being around until the Lord says it is my time. I will do all I have to, to make sure I am.

I recently had blood work done. I decided to include the results in this book so I could show you the results of my attitudes about what I eat. They are as follows:

My total cholesterol was 135 (normal is 50-200.
My LDL was 81 (normal is less than 130)
My HDL was 52 (normal is 35-60)
Triglycerides were 50 (Normal is 20-200)
My A1C was 5.20 (normal is 4.80-6.00)
My Blood Glucose was 93, which is normal.

They are all normal because I have done the work to make them normal. This is the way they are every time I have this done. When I take my meter in so the Dr can read it; he always tells me they are great. I did not get them saying I cannot change my eating habits.

I take cholesterol medication so why wouldn't my cholesterol levels be normal? I also take medication that helps me with my blood sugar levels. That is not the reason I have normal readings. I have normal readings because of the way I eat and take are of myself in these areas. I can get bad readings if I refuse to eat right. The medicines do not work unless I do the work necessary. I hear people say they are on the same medications as I am and it does not work for them. The first thing I ask them is what are you eating. A food high in cholesterol or sugar is going to get me high readings even though I am taking medications.

If you think, you can't go before your time keep doing the things you are in spite of what the Drs are telling you, and you will see that you can. If God would not have intervened, I would have gone before my time. "I will do anything I have to so I am here to kick your butt devil until it is God's time. If that means I have to change the way I eat so be it." Keep doing the things the Dr tells you to stop, and you will die whether it is God's time or not.

I will not allow being handicapped limit what I can do for the Lord. The place I am handicapped is in my memory and concentration. God's purpose for my life is where my handicap is. Why was God's purpose for me something that was so hard for me? Why was it not something where I did not have to be challenging my handicap?

The things you are gifted in are the things that the devil is going to fight you in. He is not going to worry too much about you in the areas you are not gifted. I am gifted with a positive, encouraging uplifting attitude. If you think the devil does not challenge me in those areas think again. That is where he challenges me the most. All he has to do to defeat me is get me to change my attitude and position. If he can do that he has me right where he wants me. He knows where I am gifted, and he fights me the hardest in those areas. He knows if you get loose he is in big trouble.

The Lord cannot use you until you are tested and found firm and unmovable in attitude and position. I am more than a conqueror. I have spent the last six year showing that I am. The devil fears my attitudes because I have shown him he has to.

Over and over I have rewritten and reread things I have written. My first book had me in tears several times when I started putting it together for publishing. I often said, "Why did you give me this purpose Lord?" I do not know anything about what I am doing. Several times I asked the Lord to send me some help. The Lord sent absolutely no one. I could never understand. Now I understand He wanted me to see what I was capable of if I would not give up. He wanted me to see and understand how not to let your limitations stop you. This is my fifth book, and I still have to go back and reread sometimes the whole book up to where I am to see if I said what I am about to say before. Let me tell you that could be very frustrating if I let it. I learned the hard way what you let you get what you don't let you don't get.

Persistence and patience has made each book easier. The difficulty of the first book prepared me and positioned me to become better at it as I go along. If you do not have persistence and patience and do not keep trying until you get it right you will never be in a position and condition so the Lord can use you.

If you let your limitations limit you, you will live within the limits of your limitations. If you have the right attitude, there are no limitations to what God can do with you. The only limitations are the limitation you put on yourself. Been there done that and I am not going there again.

Do whatever you have to do to be in the condition and position so the Lord can use you as He planned. That includes eating right and exercising like I have to, so I am here kicking the devils' butt until it is God's time for me to go.

THANKS I NEEDED THAT

I wish I would not have had to go through recovery to learn who I am and what I am in God's plan for my life. God did not cause the heart attack. It was my fault. He used it to get me to stop going around the same mountain of fear and doubt over and over again. And for that I have to say, "Thanks Lord, I needed that."

I needed something as tough as recovery to toughen me up. Recovery was a time the Lord was using to bring me to an understanding of all the things He put in me to fulfill my purpose. For that I have to say, "Thanks Lord, I needed that." I needed the Lord to take me through months of recovery instead of healing me instantly. If He would have healed me right away, and I would have gone back to work what I have in me would not be in me like it is.

The things that are in me to fulfill God's purpose for my life are in me because of what He has taken me through. You are prepared and positioned for what the Lord has for you to do by the things you go through. As you go through the tough times, you have to understand that the Lord is preparing and positioning you, or often you will be defeated by what you are going through.

The way you go through what the Lord takes you through is determined by your attitude. You have to have a positive, patient persistent attitude towards what the Lord is taking you to in spite of what He is taking you through.

You are going to go through many rough things to get to what the Lord is taking you to. That's the way it works. If there is no rough there is no tough. And if you are not tough the Lord cannot use you like He purposed.

The Lord cannot take me to the next level until I do what I have to get there. If I would have sat here with the attitude, " You just don't understand how hard this is. You don't understand how I feel." I would have gone nowhere, and I would have learned nothing. Was it hard for me? It was hard like I never felt in my life. Did I ever feel like doing the things I needed to? No I felt absolutely terrible. It was a terrible that is beyond words. Lousy or not I was determined that I was going to defeat the devil this time.

There were many things I did not even attempt the first year of recovery. I knew I was not physically in a condition where I could do certain things Yet. I never let that get me down. I knew with patience and persistence I would be in a position and condition to do those things again.

I might fall down or get knocked down. I learned the hard way that the only time you are beat is when you stay down. After I was knocked down I would get back up and say, "Thanks devil I needed that to wake me up to some new truths the Lord is trying to teach me. I have so much to be thankful to you for devil. The things you brought to defeat me during my time of recovery are the very things that have shown me the attitude I got through the way I was taught. So thanks devil I needed that. I am where I am in God's plan because when you tested me; I showed you I am still right here. I have to thank you for all the opportunities you have given me during the last six years. I wrote and published the books you said I could not write. I love it when you tell me I can't do something the Lord purposed me to do. You have been there all the way trying to stop me. All I have to say is thanks, I needed that."

When you are moving into the Lord's purpose, there is going to be resistance from the devil like you never felt before. The way to beat that is give the devil persistence like he never felt before. The only way to overcome the devil's resistance is to persist, persist, persist and having done all to persist keep right on persisting. The only way you can lose is if you stop persisting.

As soon as you set yourself in a positive attitude and position the devil is going to test you to see how firm and fixed in attitude you are. If you move, then God cannot move you to a higher level. If you refuse to move get ready you past the test, and you are going to a higher level.

When you are being tested is not the time to be worried and stressed. It is a time to be excited that the Lord is allowing you to go through it so that you can show the devil who you are and what you are in spite of where you are in the test. If you pass you are going to a new level, if you do not you are going to go around the same mountain again. Been there and have done that over and over again.

It's Up To You

It's up to you how you face life and its difficulties. You can handle them in a positive way or a negative way. The way you look and think about difficulties is the way you live them. I lived most of my life looking at the negative and living it. I can tell you from experience that the positive way is more fun. It also makes it stress and anxiety free. God has everything under control what in the world do I have to be stressed about?

What the devil brings to defeat us can only work on us when we start dwelling on it. "What you are saying devil could possibly be true. Yeah I will probably fail if I try. And then I will look like a fool." That was always my attitude. Therefore, it was my life. I got what I thought, and I possessed what I confessed. What did I expect?

What the devil brings to defeat us the Lord will always use to position us. It is not up to the devil, and it is not even up to the Lord. It is totally up to us. If you want to keep living a negative life keep looking at things in a negative way. If you want to live a positive victorious life always look for the message that is in the mess you are in.

I have gone through six years of recovery up to this point. I say up to this point because it will be an ongoing thing for the rest of my life.

There are things I will never gain back. I wish I would have learned what I learned in an easier manner.

The devil will try to see if he can get you to believe you are not what God says you are. To see if you really think you can do what God purposed. All he has to do is get you to doubt just a little bit, and he's gotcha right where he wantscha.

The minute you step out of the devil's way you are in your way of receiving all the Lord has for you. It is not hard to beat the devil. It is in my book the easiest thing. I can tell you how. STAY POSITIVE AND NEVER GIVE UP OR GIVE IN. The minute you give up and give in you are giving way for the devil to defeat you. If you give place, he will take that place and use it against you any way he can. When you give place, you are putting yourself in a place that can allow the things you are fearing to happen.

I went through a lot of battles because of doubt and fear, and I learned a lot in those battles. My problem was not that I did not learn what God was teaching me. It was I was not using it. In spite of what I learned I went away saying I cannot be the person you say I am Lord. That is just not me. I am to shy and timid.

After the heart attack, I finally started standing up for myself. I said, " We are not going around this mountain of fear, doubt and being timid again." I started using the challenging attitude we all must have if we are going to beat Satan. Talk back to the devil if you want to beat him. Don't just pray about it, do something about what he is trying to do in your life.

I did not recover like I have because I spent a lot of time in prayer. In fact, I did not pray much about my recovery. I got up and went and did the things I needed to do. I gain strength physically, mentally and spiritually when I do the things I must. It is not up to the Lord how much strength I gain it is always up to me. I am where I am because of what I have done to get here. If you want to irritate the devil always look at the positive side of what you are going through. He will not know what to do with you. Actually, there is nothing he can do to defeat you.

The Lord will never give up on you. The only way His plans for your life can fail is if you give up. To give up means acknowledging defeat by way of leaving the battle. To give in means to acknowledge defeat; to yield. It means to give in to the thinking saying and doing that the devil brings to defeat you. When you give in you are then in the position that you are living the defeated life the devil wants you to live. "I have been there and done that, and we are not going there again devil. You got my word because this time I am standing on The Word. And this time I gotcha right where I wantcha."

You might say; "Yeah but you don't understand what I am going through. You don't understand my circumstance." Yeah but is a very bad attitude to have. You are giving place for the devil to work and use your circumstances against you. You must learn to operate in who you are and what you are in spite of the circumstances. If you don't what you are going through is going to keep you from what God is taking you to.

It is up to you how you use the circumstances. If you allow it God will always use them to teach us and train us for what He is taking us to. The devil brings negative circumstances to make us give up and give in. The Lord uses them to promote us to higher levels. Negative circumstances are nothing to fear. They are opportunities for us to show the devil we know who and what we are in Christ. They are opportunities to become stronger and tougher. Rough circumstances will always make you tough. Rough circumstances just means the Lord is getting ready to take you higher and farther in His plans. You must stay and pass His test, or you are going around the same mountain again.

It has been up to me how I use my disabilities. I can use them against me in the devils plan for my life, or I can use them for me in the Lords plans for my life. They can be used to strengthen me or weaken me. It is up to me.

I chose to use the fact that I had to go back and forth and do things over and over again as a tool to make me stronger. The short distances I use to walk around the neighborhood are now to the other end of town. The things I had so much trouble remembering I can remember with ease. I still have a long way to go; I am gaining ground in that area not losing it. Things the devil use to bring to defeat me don't bother me any more. I just say; "do you actually think that is going to work on me? I can't believe how stupid you are devil."

It Was Still In Me

After I came back to the Lord, I realized God's Word and plans were still alive in my heart. I started to realize who I was and what I was. It took me a while to learn what I was though. The Lord kept giving me people to talk to on the internet. They would talk to me about their problems and different things they were going through. I would always ask the Lord why He was sending me these people I am not a counselor. After several months, I realized what the Lord was trying to show me. I am an encourager. Because of how I was raised; I know how to look at things in a positive encouraging way.

Sometimes I was encouraging these people when I was really messed up because of all the drugs I was on. As I encouraged them, I could barely understand them. It taught me how to act in who and what I am in spite of where I am in my recovery.

God's original purpose for my life was His final decision. The things my parents taught me are still alive in my heart. In order for them to work for me, I have to act on them.

If you ask me how I made it through these hard months of recovery I would say; "I quit acting on the things that I was thinking. I started acting on the things that were alive in my heart." God's plans for my life were not dead. God was waiting for me to come to the place where He could get me to understand who I am and what I am.

The things that we go through are not things that can destroy God's purpose for our life, unless we allow them to. You are the key not God. If God be for you, and you are not there is nothing God can do with you. It is up to you how the things you go through are used.

The Lord will never give up on you. He will make your weaknesses your strengths if you let Him. Don't let failures stop you. You may not see it but the things you have been through are the very things that God has used to prepare you and position you.

How you recover and how well you recover is all in your attitude. Your attitude must be constantly persistent and patient. Without persistence and patience, it is impossible to get all the Lord has for you.

One meaning of recovery is to restore something from an unusable state to a usable state. You should always look at recovery as something that will strengthen you and improve your condition. If you face recovery with a negative attitude, your condition is not going to improve. If you want to do all the Lord has for you to do, you are going to have to do what it takes to get there. If you want to stay where you are in a negative condition don't do anything. You get in the position so the Lord can use by doing the things necessary to get in that position. Did something very useable come out of my recovery? It absolutely did. Am I in a better condition and position to serve the Lord? I am in the best condition I have ever been.

It does not matter what you are recovering from or what you are going through as you recover. Recovery is a challenge, and you must face it with a challenging attitude. Challenging circumstances are opportunities to show who and what we are in spite of where we are in recovery.

I have just started my seventh year in recovery. I have not spent anytime in doubt and fear. I showed the devil how I would handle the challenge. You might say you sure do talk a lot about the devil. I will tell you if you do not learn to talk back to him; you are never going to make it. I did not have to go looking for the Lord or the devil during recovery. They were both there all the time. How I recovered depended on which one I was listening to.

The devil is not going to go anywhere when you are trying to go deeper in the things of God. When he is fighting you, the hardest is the time to be more persistent and determined to get all God has for you. There is a song that we used to sing in church that had the lyrics "Don't Give Up On The Edge Of A Miracle." Lots of times we lose because we give up and give in when it gets rough. When it is rough is the time when you must show the devil how tough you are.

There have times when it seems like nothing is happening. I know and understand that the Lord is positioning things, so they will be in position when the time comes to do exactly what He promised they would do.

You must learn to act in patience. The time is coming when the Lord is going to do exactly what He said. Why should I be discouraged by what I see? What I see has nothing to do with what the Lord promised.

As long as we keep the right attitudes the Lord will use our set-backs as set-ups. The only way they can become set-backs is if we have that kind of attitude about them.

Don't Be Discouraged By Small Victories

Allow the small victories to encourage you to work harder to get to the bigger ones. One day at a time is all you have to worry about. My biggest victory at first was that I could stand up for any length of time.

Recovery is a step by step level by level process that takes time. Working hard at the lesser levels relentlessly and persistently is what gets you in the condition and position so you are prepared for the higher levels. If I let the lower levels discourage me or cause me to give up or give in I will never be in the condition or position for the higher levels. It is hard to look at how hard you have worked and see what little you have gained. I often thought it would be easier to give up. Why work so hard to gain it back when I can live comfortably at this level? Would I have been comfortable at the level I was at? No I tried to persuade the Lord to let me live quietly in my old age. Let me be happy volunteering to do something at the church. I made myself available but it never worked out. If I was being a volunteer of some sort at church I would not have been challenging my handicap. In the end how much fun can that be? I enjoy sitting down and pushing hard against the difficulties that my handicaps exert on me. If it is not a fight, I cannot see how it could be that much fun.

It is hard to work through the lack of concentration that I deal with all the time. When I look at what I need to do to get where I want to go it looks to hard when I look at the entire picture. I never look at the entire picture. I do what I can and do not worry about tomorrow. I know that the victory, I have today added to the victories I have as I go along will eventually get me to where I am going. As soon as something gets too difficult for my brain that day I stop. I come back the next day and do as much as I can. Do that for as long as it takes, and you will always reach your goal. If you have the right attitude about it, you will have a lot of fun along the way. It is never easier when you give up or give in. The Lord says I am, and I can. I know what it feels like to live a life of I am not, and I can't. It is a tormented life that is very depressing.

Tell me I can't do something because of my disabilities, and I am going to show you; I can because of them. It might be one small victory at a time. That does not matter. It will be done. I know my gift, and I know it does not work until I do.

When you give up or give in you have to deal with the consequences. In church, I thought it would be easier for me if I stayed in the back where no one would notice me. The problem with that is as long as the devil has you in that condition and position he does not have to take notice of you. Always remember the position you take will determine your condition.

The word notice in this sense of the word means to pay attention to. It means to acknowledge. The word acknowledge means to admit to be real. Synonyms of the word are to concede, confess and to agree with. The devil or no one else had to notice me; I was in the back conceding, confessing and agreeing with what I thought of myself.

I now use the word in the positive sense. It means to serve notice that you are someone he needs to take notice of. He has to because you know who you are and how to operate in who you are in the Lord. When I refuse to give up it makes it easier for me and harder for the devil. As long as I stay firmly fixed in who and what I am in spite of where I am it is easy.

The word consequences means you have to deal with the aftermath. You have to deal with the effect giving up has on your life. You have to deal with the repercussion it has on your life. Repercussions means you have to deal with impact and influence. You will pay for giving up in a big way. I have been there and done that. I will never allow myself to be in that condition and position again.

The hardest class for me in school was English. Creative writing papers were papers I never turned in. Standing up in class to give a report were days I did not show up. I thought it would be easier to give up. If I did go to school, the night before I was supposed to turn in an English paper or give an oral report I always received a positive encouraging pep talk from my parents. The talks did not work because I would either skip that class or refuse to turn in the paper. I thought getting a failing grade is a lot easier than making a fool out of myself.

I was classified as one of the schools wimps because I would always run from a fight. A wimp means you are a coward, a chicken and a mommas' boy. A coward means you are a person who is scared, and easily intimidated. A chicken is a person who is afraid to try. A synonym for chicken is a quitter. It was easier to allow people to call me a wimp than it was to stand up for myself.

Was I a momma's boy? I always ran to momma for help? When I went to momma, she did not criticize me or put me down. She constantly put encouragement and positive attitudes in me. I did not use them, so they did not work. I worked the shy and timid attitudes not the ones my momma taught. I was never beaten up. I never stayed long enough. I was too busy running to momma.

It is not easier when you give up it is harder. Do you want to live with the effect giving up will have on your life? Or do you want to live with the effects never giving up will have on your life? Do you want to make it hard on yourself and easy for the devil? Or do you want to make it impossible for the devil and easy on yourself?

Being what the Lord has purposed me to be is the easiest thing

I have ever done. "That's the way I am devil so deal with it. I finally gotcha right where I wantcha."

Does the devil try me? Yes, he does constantly. When he says something, I ignore him and do the opposite. Do the opposite and you will defeat him every time What's so hard about that?

Keep Trying Until You Don't Have To Try Anymore

The things that were hard for in the beginning are not hard anymore. If fact most of the time I do them without thinking about it. I am in this condition because I worked very hard to get into this condition and position.

I had to put so much effort in my walks at the beginning. I had to go out and try to walk a mile. Now if I need to walk a mile, I do not have to try anymore. I have that because I kept trying, until now, I do not have to try to do it anymore.

I don't try to be the person the Lord purposed me to be. I know who I am and what I am, so I have a lot of fun being that person. I do not forget things when I go to the store. I go get what I need and leave. I no longer have to do things over and over again. If it needs to be done I do it without all the over and over.

I do not sit down and try to write. I do it without effort. I know that it is a gift that works perfectly when I sit down and start acting in it. "We got all the trying hard out of the way when I was writing the first book didn't we devil?"

Now that I understand who and what I am it is easy being me. It was hard when I lived in negative attitudes about myself. Is it hard being you? What are you thinking and saying about yourself. Believe in yourself. Your negative thinking saying and then doing is the only thing that can defeat you. The devil can't he only has is the power you give him.

"It's easy being me so deal with it devil. I finally gotcha right where I wantcha. I am not going anywhere and anything you bring to defeat me is going to go anywhere."

Nuclear Stress Test

I have taken this test two different times. It is a test they use to see how the stress of exerting yourself affects your heart. As it is with any procedure, they schedule you for a couple of months away. I often wonder if that is part of the test. During that wait, you get to think and worry (if you want to) about what they will find.

In the days leading up to the test and especially the night before you should have heard the devil. Trust me when you are going through a test the devil is going to throw anything and everything he can at you. He wants to get your mind off of the promises of God and on the circumstances.

He told me they were going to find something wrong. And then I would be in the hospital again. I was not worried or stressed the day of the test. I was not thinking I will probably have to stay in the hospital. I was thinking and proclaiming that I was going to walk in have the test then I was going to walk out.

The days before the stress test I walked two miles several times. People that have a problem with their heart can't do that so why am I going to let the devil, and his big mouth get me stressed and worried? I actually decided not to take this test when they set it up for me the first time. The devil would not shut up when I canceled so I said; "Ok to show you there is nothing wrong I will take it."

I am not saying ignore the symptoms. I follow my doctors orders religiously. If there is something wrong he fixes it. In the mean time when I know it is just the devil trying to get me worried and stressed I am going to stand up to him and show him I will not believe his lies.

I realized as I was going through all these tests, there was something else going on. As they were testing my heart, the Lord was testing my attitudes. The testing of my attitudes determined if there were any blockages that are in the way of the Lord doing what He has purposed in my life. I look at the last eight or nine months of tests as a stress test that the Lord is allowing me to go through to see if things that should stress me do. If I allow them to the Lord sees He has to do more work in my life.

As I went through the stress test on my heart there was also a stress test going on in my life. I had a family situation going on that I am not free to talk about at this time. Also at the same time, my daughter found out, there was something wrong in her pregnancy. I know this is just a test that will put us in the right position, so we trust the Lord like we were purposed to.

Absolute trust in the Lord is the way you battle any stress your circumstances bring against you. None of this stressed me. The positive, encouraging uplifting words come out of my mouth in spite of anything I may be going through.

I passed the Dr's stress test and went home with nothing wrong just like I was expecting. Gotcha again devil! I don't care what the devil brings I will not allow it to stress me. The Lord has it under control what do I have to be stressed about? That has always been my attitude and that will continue to be my attitude.

BREAKTHROUGH

Break through means the act of overcoming or penetrating an obstacle or restriction. To overcome, to prevail over, to gain the victory, to conqueror by the power of the Holy Spirit that is within you. There will never be a breakthrough until you start doing the things that are going to cause you to breakthrough.

The breakthroughs that have came in my recovery have been because I did the things I had to in spite the difficulty. Always going one step farther today than I did yesterday. I had them because I put actions with my prayers. I was going to get it, and nothing was going to stop me. So often we don't have one because we give up and give in to soon. We don't stick with it until we are successful in overcoming.

The Lord gave me more chances than I can count to overcome my shy, fearful attitudes. I never could because if things got to hard I never stayed until I had a breakthrough. I always left in doubt and fear. The reason I finally broke through is because this time, I stayed and broke through all that nonsense in my life.

You may be in a mess of your own making. If you stay and don't run in doubt and fear the Lord will make your mess into a message that will teach you and arm you for the plans He has for your life.

The Lord had to take me back and forth over and over again

through the same kind of battle until I finally understood. I have always had the teaching and training and even the attitudes in me to become the conqueror I am today. I was not using it like the Lord purposed me to.

My breakthroughs came because the heart attack helped me see what the Lord, my parents and everyone else was trying to teach me. I thought I was a pretty weak person. The heart attack brought out the tough in me that the Lord and everyone else was trying to get out of me. The comment I heard before was I was a weak nobody. The comment I hear since the heart attack is you are so tough.

The reason I am is because I took all that my parents put in me and the gifts the Lord put in me and broke through all the devils nonsense to become the person I am today. There will be no breakthrough until you start thinking saying and doing the things that will cause you to become the person the Lord purposed you to be.

Recovery has been constantly breaking through difficulties to overcome the disabilities they said I would have. I had to breakthrough many difficulties to understand and relearn how to do things all over again. I relearned them because I never gave up or gave in until I broke through and am doing those things once again.

Want a breakthrough? You have to think, say and do the things that will cause you to. That is the only way. One of the first things the Lord said to me at the beginning was; "Don't just pray about it do something about it."

PATIENCE IS DEVELOPED
THROUGH PRESSURE

If there is one thing recovery will develop in you, it is patience. It will teach you patience, or else it will get you stressed and anxious. At first, I would let things get me stressed and then I would go home the rest of the day and feel lousy because of how it made me feel.

I decided to use the stressful anxious situations to become a strong patient person. I got to the point where I would say, "I bet you think this is going to stress me don't you devil? I am going to use it to become a strong patient person. I will wait as long as it takes and will not get inpatient."

The pressure of sometimes waiting for simple little things to be done can either make me stressed and anxious, or it can make me into the patient person the Lord purposed me to be. Standing in lines forever when you can just barely stand up is a great chance to be impatient.

The pressures of our circumstances can make us or break us. They can either make us into the person the Lord purposed us to be, or they can make us into the person the devil wants us to be. We need to learn to act in spite of the circumstances instead of because of them. In spite of the circumstances, I am going to trust and believe the Lord for what He promised me. We should never think because of my circumstances I just don't know. I don't think I can make it through this.

I like getting thanked for my patience. When you are acting in patience, you are not putting any pressure on the other person to perform the way you think they should. I still have a hard time getting people to understand me because of what the heart attack did to my communication skills. It can get difficult for those I am dealing with if I come at them with an impatient attitude. I do my best to come at them with a very patient attitude. I always let them understand that I have disabilities, so I am not going to understand easy. I like people to like my attitude and be encouraged so that is the kinds of attitudes I use. Your negative attitudes will not return unto you void. Negative attitudes and words have a negative affect in the situation. Positive words have positive affect.

When you go to the doctor for tests most of the time, there is a long, and I do mean long wait. A few times I lost my cool and would give them a piece of my mind. That really didn't help. It made me feel bad for giving a piece of my mind instead of the peace of my mind. The way I found to make people more willing to go out of their way to help is always acting with the peace of my mind. When I go out of my way to project the peace of my mind, their attitude changed toward me.

I did not wake up and suddenly become a patient person. It was a decision I used to make me into the person I am today. I still get impatient about some things occasionally. I am working on that. Considering the way I use to be I am a very patient person now.

According To Your Faith

Matthew 9:29 says "According to your faith so be it unto you." Our faith in the Lord and ourselves determines what the Lord can do for us and through us.

When it came to things I knew the Lord purposed me to do I had no faith in myself. There was no faith in the Scriptures that were being quoted to me. I realize now that I am full of them. Being full of them and acting on them are two different things. Before the heart attack, I could quote them to you and tell you exactly where to find them. I could even tell you how to act on them even though I wasn't.

I coulda done all the things the Lord purposed me to do if I would have believed in myself. No weapon formed against me would have prospered if I would not have let it. According to my faith so was it unto me. I had no faith in myself so that's the way it was for me.

You can go to church and hear the most inspiring faith-filled message and still go home defeated. If you do not take the words and The Word, you are hearing and act on them, it will not work for you. If you have more faith in the problem than you do in The Word. So be it unto you. If it is in failure, you will fail because that is where your faith is. That's the way you are thinking, saying and acting.

I can't was one of my hang ups. My faith was not in the Lord or in myself; it was in the fact that I had the attitude of, I can't. If it looked to hard I would leave in defeat. Even though the Lord said I could and those who were encouraging me said I could. You can succeed and do a good job and still think you failed. I have done this all my life. I was a preacher's kid and had many opportunities to speak in church. Sometimes I was brave and tried. I was complimented on how well I did. I never thought I did good though. I always retreated to my old way of thinking. There is no way I can do that. It's just not me. I am to shy was the attitude that kept me from becoming a minister. My faith was in being shy and thinking that's just not me. I failed because as my faith was so was it for me.

The devil told me all the time I would fail and not make it through recovery. I let him know from the start that this time, I have more faith in the Word and myself than he could hope to handle. I never struggled was stressed or anxious about anything. I have to deal with mental disabilities. I mean they have to deal with my attitude about them. It has never stopped me from doing what I know the Lord purposed me to do and it never will.

"As my faith is so be it unto me and as my faith is so be it unto you devil. I finally gotcha right where I wantcha and you are not going anywhere in my life because I am not going anywhere. I am still right here persisting to all the Lord has for me."

Yeah but you don't understand my circumstances. You don't know my situation. You don't understand the family member that is giving me all this trouble. Is your faith in your circumstances and your situation? Or is it in the Lord? Is your faith in what you see or is it in the Lord? Acts 16:31 Says, "Believe in the Lord and you and your household will be saved." Why did the heart attack not kill me? I was deep in sin when it happened. There is no doubt in my mind that my parents standing on this verse saved me from hell. It was not luck I survived it was my parent's prayers. As their faith was so was it be unto them. I will be in heaven with them someday.

In spite of all the back and forth I never wavered in my attitudes about myself. I never stayed in bed worrying or feeling sorry for myself. I always got out of bed and showed the devil I would do what

I had to do to make it through the day. I have shown him I would do whatever I had, to so I would recover all the things I lost.

My daughter was pregnant and when they did tests they found fluid where it should not be. They said the baby might be handicapped. I encouraged her and gave her the scripture Matthew 18:19 which says, "That if any two of you agree as touching any one thing, it shall be done for them by the father in heaven." We were both agreeing and praying that they would find nothing when they did further tests. When they did they found nothing. In fact, the second Doctor was trying to figure out what the first doctor was looking at when he saw the fluid. There was nothing there it was perfectly normal as we agreed in prayer. As our faith was so was it unto us.

We could have spent the time awaiting for the birth worried and stressed. Why would we do that? It is more fun standing in faith with full assurance that as we agreed, it would be done unto us. Instead of a handicapped baby, she had a normal baby.

When you are in doubt and fear you give the devil something to work with. When you stay firm in faith and trust in the Lord, the devil has nothing to work with. How is he going to defeat you if you are not worried?

HAVE FAITH IN YOURSELF

Have faith in yourself and your abilities. Whether you succeed or not depends upon your attitude about your abilities. Without faith in yourself, you will never make it to the marvelous heights the Lord wants to take you. Having faith in yourself is having trust and confidence in the magnificent gifts the Lord put in you. It is having confidence in the Lord as He prepares you and positions you for His purpose for your life. When the Lord gifts you, you have everything you need to fulfill His purpose. Handicapped or not you still have the gift. It is not dependent on your condition. It is dependent on your position concerning the matter.

If you have no faith in yourself, the Lord can't use the gifts. If you have confidence in failure, you will fail. That is the way you are thinking saying and doing. Why wouldn't you fail? You thought it; you got it. You confess it so you possess it and it possesses you.

I failed to become a minister because I did not have any confidence, trust or faith in myself. I do not blame anyone but myself. I do not blame the devil because he only had the power I gave him.

The word trust means you have to believe in your strengths and abilities. The word capabilities means qualities, abilities and even the personality that when developed will be used for His glory. I never liked my personality because I was a shy person. I never trusted the

Lord or myself that I could become anything else. You will live a life based upon the things you have faith in. I never had any faith in any of the positive, encouraging words I heard about myself. Mom and dad say I can and the Lord says I can, but I don't think I can. The faith you don't have in yourself will win every time. The devil has you right where he wants you.

I am a quiet person. That does not mean I am not confident in who I am. When I have recovered enough, and the Lord has me positioned right you will see I am not shy to speak it as the Lord originally intended. That is my final decision I will not give up until I am able to do that.

Be your own best friend not your own worst enemy. I just read something that is so true. "Whether you think you can or think you can't you are right." Focus on your limitations and sure enough they will limit how you live. To limit yourself is to limit what God can do in your life. I did not become what the Lord originally intended because I allowed limitations I thought I had control my life.

When the Lord created you, you came fully loaded with all you will ever need to fulfill His plans in your life. The devil knows that, and that's where he will be constantly. If He can get you to think, you are not, and you can't he's gotcha. You can do all the things the Lord purposed and gifted you to do. Believe in yourself and you will not believe what the Lord will do through you. Take the "t" off of can't and show the devil you can, and you will.

I like being me. I am a very positive person. I like being my own best friend instead of always my worst enemy. I like being a quite person. It makes it easy for me to be patient and trust in the Lord. It is so easy being me now that I understand why God made me the way He did. The personality the Lord gave me fit's the purpose He has for me perfectly.

You will live up to your expectations. If you don't expect very much of yourself that is how you will live. Your thoughts, your words and your actions will be full of what you expect. The word expect means to look forward to. If you are looking forward to and seeing nothing but failure and defeat what are you expecting? What are you thinking and saying about yourself?

Very early in my recovery the Lord told me to talk to myself. To say wonderful encouraging, positive things to myself. He told me to stop using the word can't and start using the words I am; I can therefore, I will. During the hardest days of recovery, I never used the word can't. The word can't has the power of the attitude behind it. It was always and will always be, "I am; I Can and there is nothing in the world or hell that will stop me."

I am thankful for the back and forth and over and over that I had to do. That is where I gained the strength to become what I am today. Back and forth over and over just means stronger and stronger and better and better. My writing is better because I have relentlessly done it over and over until it got better.

I finally have faith in myself. I see that I have the attitudes, the persistence, the patience and the personality to become what the Lord purposed me to be. I might make mistakes that does not mean I am going to quit trying. That just means I am going to keep trying until I succeed.

I just read a cute quote by an unknown person. It says, "If at first you don't succeed, do it like your mother told you." That is so true for me. If I would have kept trying like my mother told me I would have succeeded. I would have become the Minster I was purposed to be.

IF ANY TWO AGREE

Matthew 18:19 says in part, "If any two agree as touching any one thing, it shall be done by my Father in heaven." The Lord will do what we ask when we stay firm and unmovable in agreement.

I am going to discuss this from the negative angle to show you how agreeing with the wrong people and the wrong things can defeat you. If the other one you are agreeing with is the devil you open the door to him. My faith was always agreeing with what he said to me. "You are a nobody, no one's going to listen to you." I believed him so as my faith was I was.

The word agree means to give consent, accede, allow and comply. To comply means to act in accordance with, to yield and conform to. When you are agreeing with the negative, you are giving it consent to work in your life. To give consent means to give permission and to allow.

When you comply you act like the person you think you are. You will stay within the safety net of only doing the things you know you can. I know from experience that you will act out the negative that is going on in your mind.

When you give up on the plans, the Lord has for your life, there is nothing the Lord can do with you. You are the key to His plans. When you leave in defeat like I always did you will live in defeat like

I did. How can the Lord get you in a position so He can use you if you always quit and leave when it gets hard? I learned the hard way that the tough is in the rough. When you leave you are not allowing the Lord to make you the tough person He wants you to be. You are abandoning hope that you can or will ever be that person.

When you give up you are giving way for the devil to move in and defeat the plans the Lord has for your life. After I gave up and left Bible school I was drafted into the army. I stopped serving the Lord and started doing the things of the world. The sex addiction I suffered with most of my life got in me in the service.

The ministry of faith and encouragement the Lord had for me; I gave up for a life of doubt and fear. There were times during my life when I was serving the Lord. For the most part, I had longer periods when I was not serving the Lord. Even when I was serving the Lord I was not living the victorious life, He purposed me to live.

I had wonderful Christian parents. They were always positive and encouraging. My momma, in particular, was my biggest encourager. No matter what she saw in me; she was always positive and encouraging. She put it in me, so I had it in me to become what I was purposed to be. My problem was not that I did not have it. It was that I did not believe what I had. The two that were in agreement in my life were not me and my momma. It was me and the devil.

When you agree with the negative that the devil or others say about you, you are giving it power to work in your life. When I chose to agree with the devil and not my positive encouraging momma. I gave the devil the power to run my life. As my faith was so was it unto me.

The only thing I had to do when I turned my life around was to stop agreeing with the devil and start believing what my momma taught me. Now the two that are agreeing are me and my momma. Now I understand and agree with her. The prayers she prayed over me were there just waiting for me to agree and become what we all knew I was purposed to be.

There may be those that read this that are discouraged because you never agreed with the prayers your parents prayed over you.

The prayers your parents prayed did not fall on deaf ears. They have been following you waiting for you to agree. The moment I started agreeing with what the Lord and my momma said I started becoming victorious. When I say, "I am, I Can, therefore, I will," I am agreeing with what the Lord says I am. In my mind, I am also agreeing with momma.

The things that life brings and the things the devil brings to defeat you only have power when you agree. Many days in the early stages of recovery I had to disagree with my circumstances. I told the devil day after day that in spite of the circumstances I would do what I had to. One of the synonyms of spite is to annoy. To annoy means to be bothersome and troublesome and be downright irritating.

My attitude was always I can agree with you devil, or I can disagree and be nothing but trouble. I turned my life around by not agreeing with him and all the negative thoughts I had about myself.

To Agree With

What you agree with you agree to. It would be easy to agree with my handicaps. They are not visible. That makes it hard because I always have to stop and explain to people why I am having a hard time with the things they are explaining to me. The hardest thing for me to overcome was my lack of concentration. It causes me to ask the same question repeatedly. I learned if I am not careful this can make others stressed with me. Not to mention what it could do to me if I let it.

There is no reason I should not have gotten lost when I went for walks. The reason I did not was because I told the devil, I would not allow him to do that to me. He constantly said; "You will fall down and there will be no one to help you." I disagree based on Psalms 91:11-12. Verse 11 says in part, "He gives His angels charge over us." Verse 12 says, "They will bear you up lest you dash your foot against a stone." A couple of other translations say, "so that you won't dash your foot against a stone." One puts it, "so that you won't even hurt your foot on a stone." Even though I felt like it most of the time the first year of recovery I never fell down or got lost. These verses worked for me because I was not afraid to put the force of my determination to work.

Not only did I have to tell the enemy I disagreed. I also had to show him. When you start agreeing with the devil or anyone, you are agreeing to that kind of defeated life. Your disabilities only have the power that you give them. If you want to feel sorry for yourself and give in you are agreeing to allow them to have power over your life.

When the Lord gives you the promise, it is very hard to see how you will be able to take possession of such a promise. You have to understand between promise and possession, there is a lot of persistence and patience as He prepares and positions you for possession of the promise.

I could have taken the attitude that because of my disabilities and limitations, I can't write. It is too hard to reread and rewrite things over and over again. I had to realize as I reread and rewrote it; I got better at it. Isn't that what it is all about?

The answer is not in giving up on the promise; it is in relentlessly and persistently doing whatever you have to over and over so you become better. Better only comes when you do things over and over enough to make you better at it. Don't be discouraged by back and forth and over and over it is your best friend if you use it right.

Don't agree with the devil and the limitations of your handicaps. Disagree that they can limit what you can do for God. The only limits you have are the limitations you agree with. Remember agree means compliance in response to any form of persuasion or opposition.

It is up to me how I live the rest of my life. I could live it within the limitations of my disabilities. Or I can use my limitations as a catalyst to drive me to become the person the Lord always purposed me to be.

When the Lord laid it on my heart to write I gave Him all the reasons I couldn't. Overcoming the limitations and disabilities that I have is the entry way for what the Lord has for me to do the rest of my life. If I do not face and overcome them, I can't live in the full purpose the Lord has for my life.

The full purpose the Lord has for your life is when you have done all He purposed you to do. Where you stop pursuing is where you will live. The books I have published are published because I would not be limited by my mental handicaps. When you quit trying you put limitations on what the Lord can do in your life. He may have shown you wonderful things He is going to do in your life. He can't do those things if you put limitations on Him by putting limitations on yourself.

Where are the four books, I have written available? They are available through any major online bookseller all over the world. I did not start thinking I was going to do that. I started thinking I would write a small testimony about what happened. I did not think I could write and publish a book. I don't think I even wanted to give it a try. I started to write my first book because my step mom kept encouraging me to. The power of encouragement is so powerful when you act on it.

They say I have heart disease and pre-diabetes. As far as I am concerned, I may have them, but they do not have me. I am not worried one bit about dying. I refuse to agree with letting these things limit what I can and will do for the Lord. I do the things the doctors tell me, and I trust the Lord to do the things He promised in His Word. I do not agree that I have to sit around and feel lousy all the time. You can if you want. I can tell you it is not a whole lot of fun doing it that way. The fun is in getting up and doing what you have to in spite of the circumstances. Keeping a positive attitude because you know that with your help, the Lord will work all things for your good.

Think Like It's Going To Happen

Think like it's going to happen, talk like it's going to and act like its going to. The way you think is the key to how you live. It will show in your words and actions.

When the Lord gives you a promise, and you think like it's going to happen, act like it's going to and talk like it's going to it will. Your thoughts, words and actions are based on faith in the Lord and His Word. Your actions will follow the way you are thinking.

When you are thinking and talking like it is going to happen in a negative way you are opening the door for it to happen that way. When you are thinking negative, your words will be full of the power of your negative words and your actions will give it the negative power it needs.

I did not think much of myself so that is the way I thought and acted. "I am a nobody. No one will listen to what I have to say. If I try I will fail I just know it." Why did I always fail? I thought like it, talked like it and I acted like it. What did I expect? I got what I expected.

I ran in fear sometimes just because I was thinking about what I was expecting to happen. I did because I was acting on the negative way, I was thinking and saying. Many times the bad things I thought were going to happen never did. It still kept me running in fear that they were going to. Maybe not this time but I know they will next time.

I quit jobs, lost houses and cars and even lost the Lords plans for my life. Not because bad things happened to cause it, but because of the way, I was thinking saying and doing. When you are thinking defeat, you will be talking and acting it.

Whatever you are thinking about constantly you will be talking about constantly. You are thinking about it constantly and talking about it constantly so you will be acting on it constantly. Why was I constantly defeated by doubt and fear? That is what I was thinking and talking about constantly.

Thinking like negative things are going to happen, talking like they are is putting your faith in them happening. Faith in the wrong things works just like faith in the right things. If you have enough faith in the negative, it will come to pass just like you believed it would. It will come to pass because you are acting so that it will.

I made it through a very long difficult, stressful recovery enjoying myself. Thinking, saying and acting on words that would defeat me were never allowed to cross my lips. Thinking, talking and acting on all the negative I was up against would have given it power to defeat me. I never talked about what I was going through. I always talked about what I was going to. Back and forth over and over I don't care how hard it is or how long it takes. Don't talk about the problem talk to the problem.

My mental handicaps make it some of the mechanics of writing are hard. The devil constantly tells me to give up. Do I feel like giving up sometimes? Yes, I do. Do I think about giving up? Yes, I do. Do I ever say or act like I am going to? No I will never give up. The only days I do not write are the two days my wife has off from her job. All the other days I am still right here writing like I know the Lord purposed. I know how it feels to give up on the plans the Lord has for your life. I will never give up again.

You are the key to what the Lord can do in your life. Be careful what you are thinking and saying about what the Lord can do through you. If you are thinking, saying and doing the wrong things, you will never get in position, so He can use you. If you are thinking, saying and doing the things that are going to get you into the position and condition, so He can use you He will. The only limits to how the Lord can use you are the limits you put on yourself.

Your attitude determines the altitude the Lord can take you in His plans for your life. You can do none of what the Lord purposed. You can do some of what He purposed, or you can have the attitude that I will do all of things the Lord purposed. It is up to you.

ALL THING WORK FOR YOUR GOOD

Recovery has been a rewarding time. I can honestly say that everything I went through has worked for my good. I need to make it understood though that it worked that way because I worked it that way. Things would not have worked for the good if I did the wrong things. I have done that all my life, so I know what I am talking about.

In the past most of the time after I quoted this scripture I would go out and do something that was not going to work for my good. Thinking faith, talking faith and then acting negative does not work. It does you no good to speak it and talk it and then run from the things you fear. I have given positive encouraging talks in church that were inspiring. After them, I would go right back to acting negative. What good did that do me? Your thinking, saying and then doing have to be going the same direction.

Nothing I have been through would have worked for my good without my participation. Praying by itself would not have worked. I know for a fact that you can pray that all things work for your good and then act so they will not. Pray then act so that they will is the only way it will work.

The difficulty that I have been through could have destroyed me if I had the wrong attitude. When you have the wrong attitude, you will have the wrong action. When you have the wrong action you cannot expect for it to work for your good. The way you expect things to work is the way you can expect them to. During recovery I never start anything with the expectation that I will fail. I know from experience that does not work for my good. I expect that in the end, I will succeed. I know that all things will work for my good because I make sure they do. Between the promise and possession of the promise is a lot of no give up no give with patient persistence.

I tend to get excited when a situation comes along that seems too hard. I know because of my attitude it is going to make me strong. It does not matter how I feel my actions will be the ones that take me to the altitude I have determined I will go. Attitude always determines altitude. Your attitude always determines your actions. And your actions determine how things work for you. Our attitude should never be why me? Why do I have to go through this? The Lord would never allow it if He did not know it was going to work out for your good.

Not everything needs our physical action. Sometime it is our actions of faith and trust in the Lord. Not worrying about things when I have physical things I am dealing with is an act of faith. Not worrying about medical bills is an action of faith and trust that the Lord has things under control. I can never understand why I should be stressed.

The secret is doing it over, and over, and over and over and over and over and over and over and over and over until you succeed. Have no consideration for how hard it is. You will go to amazing altitudes because you have the right attitude and actions to get you there. With the right attitude the challenge triggers the power within you.

THE CHALLENGE TRIGGERS
THE POWER

The challenge of the lengthy recovery was the thing that triggered the power of the wonderful things in me. I would not have learned these things without a lengthy recovery period. My thinking was this knocked me down, but it did not knock me out. I am still here. I will take the things I learned in a wonderful Christian home and use them like I should have.

Every time I felt like it was going to be too hard it triggered a determination in me that was going to show that I could with no concern for the challenge. The harder it was the more fun it was in my book.

Challenge it and it will change. When you give in to your circumstances, nothing is going to change. You will be at the same level tomorrow that you are today. I woke up often thinking I don't feel like I am going to make it through this day. I went to bed every day proud of myself because I showed that I could face the challenge and win. I was never at the same level of recovery the next day because I made sure that I was not. One step farther today means I was at a level of recovery that I was not at yesterday.

The definition of the word challenge that I like is to demand as something rightful yours. A great recovery is mine because I am not going to settle for anything less. Anything that challenges it will trigger the power of the determination that is in me.

The challenge triggers what I allow it to. I can remember days when the enemy said if you sit down and write you will fail miserably. That did not trigger agreement. It triggered the power of determination and persistence. The days I felt like that are the days I wrote the most. Those were the days I sat down at the computer and started writing, which then triggered the gift that is in me.

There is something about feeling like it is impossible that I love. If it seems impossible bring it on. Showing you that it is not is the fun part. The doctors said it would be impossible for me to survive what I went through and not be in a vegetative state of mind. The Lord prevented that. He did not prevent me from being in a handicapped state of mind. He knew that having to deal with that challenge was going to be the thing that triggered me to start using all the wonderful things in me.

I know I am still here because the Lord is not through with me yet. I will show you I know it. I write because I know it is the Lord's purpose for my life. The fun part of it is I get to challenge the limitations of my disabilities daily as I do it. The power of the gift of writing that is in me is not triggered until I sit down and take the position at the computer. I almost never know what I am going to write until I take the position.

You cannot let self-doubt, and fear trigger the wrong actions and expect to live a victorious life. The challenge before me in the early days of recovery is what made me get up and do the things I did not feel like doing.

The power of my determination and persistence's lies in the fact that I know it is empowered by the Holy Spirit that is within me Acts 1:8. When I act with determination and persistence, I know that I will succeed because it is not just my determination and persistence that I am acting on. I am acting so that the power of the Holy Spirit that is in me can work.

The anger I have in my heart towards what I let the devil do is the thing that triggers and propels me to work so hard to do the things I coulda and shoulda done long ago. I let the enemy take my ministry. I will show him that in spite of my disabilities, I will take it back. I might add I will love every minute of it.

The Steps Of A Good Man

Psalms 37:23 says in part; "The steps of a good man are ordered by the Lord." You mean to say that the bad steps I made were ordered by the Lord? The bad steps I made that led to the failures taught me the things I know today. It has given me the experience and understanding of the things of God that I have. Looking back at my life and seeing the times I gave up and the consequences I paid has given me the drive I have.

God will allow you to go through things of your own making to try to get you in the position, He needs you to be to use you. I wish I would not have went through the things I did. I know that in my failures there have been lessons, I would not have learned any other way. I see the hand of God in every one of them.

The determination I have came from giving in all the time. The consequences I paid are something that I refuse to have to deal with again. Paying those consequences is the trigger behind my determination. To say that God was not there all the time teaching me valuable lessons would be wrong.

To all the bullies, I ran from when I was a kid I have to say thank you. I needed that to build me into the person I am today. Feeling I was a nobody that no one would listen to has given me the drive I needed. I will show you I am a somebody who has a lot to say.

When you are a failure all of your life, it is easy to think you have nothing to give. The truth is you are the people that have the most to give. You have the experience of the consequences of your failures to use to teach others. So that they will not make the same mistakes you did. If they have made the same mistakes, you can show them they have so much to give that will be a big help to others in the same position.

Do you have heart disease and diabetes? Do you have to have expensive test done on a frequent basis? I wish I did not have these things to deal with. I have to say that having to deal with them has made me into the person I am. I get to show on a constant basis the determined, persistent attitude that is in me. I get to show the faith I have in myself and God on a constant basis.

I have a lot of expensive procedures and tests done yet I have no big medical bills to deal with. They are not my problem, they are the Lords. I know who I am and whose, I am I refuse to worry about anything.

When I make a mistake because of my mental disabilities, the Lord is there to pick me up. When He picks me up it is my job to stay in faith, persistence and determination and to keep right on going.

Part of the reason I can do what I do like I do is because of my disabilities. I have learned that I can do all the things I am purposed to do in spite of my disabilities. In my opinion, the disability are the thing that makes it fun.

The steps of this good man have always been ordered by the Lord. That is the way it will continue to be. I am; I can and I will because of the things I have been through. Gotcha right where I wantcha devil.

The Lord Has It Covered

I depend on the Lord for the little things daily. Last night my computer and printer both started acting up. I worked on them for a little while and could not figure out what was wrong. Instead of getting stressed I decided to pray about it. After praying I tried working on the printer again. Within a few minutes, I had it working fine. It was not so with the computer. I gave it a couple of tries and told the Lord it was His problem. Today when I went on the computer it was working fine. I have no idea what was wrong. I guess I was just lucky. Yeah right!

I have a hard time communicating so I have started asking the Lord to give me the nice easy to talk to people. I had several things I needed to deal with the last few days. Every person that helped me in these matters have been the nicest people. One lady who helped me yesterday worked the whole day with me on a matter. She was a very nice sweet lady. I guess I was just lucky that I got all of these nice people to help me. I was not lucky I prayed for it and went to the appointments expecting my prayers would be answered.

This past winter we went on vacation. We had to go through security a number of times and had to switch gates quite a bit. We made a number of mistakes and ended up in the wrong place several times. The funniest thing was that in every wrong place, there was a nice person that stopped and helped us. In one airport, we spent the night sleeping at the gate written on our ticket. When we woke up there was a man that was on the same flight telling us we were at the wrong gate. Missing our flight would have been a difficult and stressful thing to deal with. Do not tell me that the Lord did not have someone at all of these places taking care of this good man. The steps of this good disabled man were ordered by the Lord even though we were in the wrong place a lot of the time. It is easy to get lost in the LA airport if you are not mentally disabled. Ask anyone who has been there. The Lord knows where I am and knows how to get me where I am going even when I have no clue.

One day we were lost in a hospital trying to figure out where we were supposed to go. A Chaplin came along and took us where we needed to go. I do not fear going where I need to because I know the Lord goes before me directing my path through other people.

Recently I discovered that I made a mistake when I signed up for my retirement insurance. I did not sign up for dental care. I made the mistake because I was not in good shape mentally at the time. I started to worry about it then the Lord said: "Haven't you learned anything? I have all the mistakes you have made covered." It will be interesting to watch how He works this one out. I mean it will be a lot of fun. The Lord has you covered there is nothing to worry about. If you want to worry it is your choice. That means He has to do more work in your life to get you to the point where you refuse to worry. I do not like going around the same mountain over and over again. I will learn the first time and save myself the hassle.

"Don't worry be happy." What do you want to do? Be happy and not worry or worry and not be happy? It is a lot more fun being happy and free of worry.

ENTHUSIASM

My days were easier when I used the right attitude with a lot of enthusiasm. I never woke up thinking "oh no" another long hard day of work to try to gain back the things I lost. A positive persist attitude with a lot of enthusiasm was a must. I knew that in the end, I was going to win.

To be perfectly honest now that I think about it, I did wake up thinking and feeling that way once in a while. Waking up thinking and feeling that way does not mean I am going to act that way. The feeling and thinking have no power unless you start acting on it.

Enthusiasm means excited interest; an eagerness to do something. Why wouldn't you be eager to work hard at something when the Lord already said you were going to win? Knowing the outcome of all of my hard work is what made it so much fun. Right devil? He, he gotcha again.

Enthusiasm is a strong excitement to go to battle. The word excitement means a pleasant anticipation or lively enjoyment of. We are more than conquerors (Romans 8:37). Why wouldn't we be eager and enthusiastic about going to battle? We get in trouble when we fear what it could do to us. We should be looking at what it can do for us. We know the outcome, as long as we stay strong in faith and action. We know it does not have any power to do anything to us, unless we let it.

As long as you stay enthusiastic, persistent and patient you should by all means get very excited about what you know the outcome will be. Eager to face whatever you need to for that day. The best days of my recovery were the days I succeeded after months of hard enthusiastic work. I Loved it when I could say to the enemy, "See I told you I could and would."

How do you stay enthusiastic and excited about your day when you don't feel like it? I have the choice about how I am going to act. I found out the hard way that you get a lot of trouble and difficulty when you act the negative way. I knew the promises I was acting on would make me victorious in spite of the way I was feeling. So when I did not feel like doing something that I knew was for my good I did it anyway. I did not do it trying to just barely make it. I did it with a lot of eager anticipation because I knew what the outcome would be eventually.

Staying positive, determined and enthusiastic about what I was doing was a must. I did not want to make my goals just barely all the time. I wanted to make them with ease. Staying enthusiastic and excited made small victories on my way to the big ones a real blast as far as I am concerned.

I learned the hard way that your biggest encourager has to be you. If you are not for you with faith persistence and enthusiasm, you are not going to win. In spite of how I feel I speak from a positive enthusiastic position. The position you take concerning a situation always determines your condition and ability to face and overcome the situation.

There are still a lot of times I have to face the limitations of my handicaps. When I face those times I do not back down and say; "Things will never change. I will always be stopped by my handicaps." When I say that I am absolutely right. It will never change, and I will always be stopped by my handicaps. There is no faith determination and enthusiasm to go on so why would it be any different than the way I am expecting? Rest assured that you can expect to live the life you are expecting. That is where your faith and actions are so that is where you are and will stay unless you change. I have years of experience I know what I am talking about.

I know the dreams the Lord put in my heart. It so often looks like they will never happen. I have faith that they are going to because I work hard with a lot of enthusiasm to get myself into position and condition so that they can. Enthusiasm is a very important part of your faith. Without it you will not successfully get things in position so the Lord can do what He wants to in your life. Trust me when I say no battle can be won without an attitude full of enthusiasm.

I never face anything with a why me attitude. I did that most of my life, and it did not get me anywhere. When I started facing things with an enthusiastic go ahead and try me attitude I started having the victories and fun that I was purposed to have.

In spite of anything you face always stay positive and enthusiastic about the wonderful things the Lord is taking you to. The most essential factor is persistence and determination. Never allow your energy or enthusiasm to be dampened by the discouragement that will inevitably try to come.

SOME FINAL ENCOURAGEMENT

The most important thing to remember in difficult circumstances is have the right attitude. That is what determines your success. The way you think can defeat you and stop you from doing anything. Most of the time you are not defeated by your circumstances. You are defeated by how you think about them.

You have to learn to think, talk and act like you are the over-comer the Lord says you are in spite of the circumstances. The word spite means regardless and in defiance of. You are only defeated when you think you are.

Believe in yourself! Have faith in your abilities! If you don't you will never reach the heights the Lord has for you. The only one that has the power to stop you is you. The devil does not have that much power. Your circumstances do not have that much power. The only power, the devil or your circumstance have is the power you give them.

All my life I never had any faith in myself or my abilities so that is the way I lived. A defeated shy nobody. I always thought and said; "If I step out in faith and act on the abilities God has given me, I will fall down." Most of the time I did because I knew I would. What did I expect?

I am not going to stay down because that would give the devil and my circumstances the power. If I step out in faith and fall down that means I am not strong enough to make it yet. I will not live like a shy nobody. I will show the devil any time he wants to try me that I am somebody he does not want to mess with. Under no circumstances will I give up, give in or back down from who and what I am.

Stand firm and do something about obstacles. You will find they are not as powerful as you think they are. They only have the power to defeat you when you think and act like they do.

The way I changed to a victorious life was I changed my thought life. I no longer think I can't, and I am not. I think I can do everything the Lord purposed me to do. I have a lot of faith in myself and my abilities.

CHANGE YOUR THOUGHTS AND YOU WILL CHANGE YOUR WORLD. So what if you failed all your life. God did not go anywhere neither did His plans for your life. You still have the abilities and gifts He put in you. All you have to do is have faith in the Lord, yourself and your abilities as He prepares you and positions you for the full purpose He has for your life.

Impossible situations are opportunities to learn to become all the Lord purposed us to be. The devil has challenged me many times during recovery. I look at those times as opportunities to show where I am and who I am in the seemingly impossible situations.

The heart attack damaged my mental capabilities to the point I had to retire and go on disability. I never look at it as a set-back? I have known from the start that it was a set-up. The Lord was giving me the opportunity to become what I was always purposed to be. If the devil or anyone else thinks they will stop me, I hope they try. When they try it gives me the opportunity to show who I am and what I am in the Lord.

Do you ever notice that negative people seem to always be in negative situations? It seems like positive people have all the luck. People attract their circumstances by their own attitudes and actions. Your negative words and actions are like a magnet that draws negative toward you. Your faith is expressed through your thoughts and words. When you are thinking negative you are seeing only the negative side of the situation. You are only looking at what the negative situation is doing to you. When you think positive you are thinking about what the situation can do for you. Your thoughts need to be what good can come from this? How can I turn this into a blessing?

Celebrate your victories. Be proud of yourself. Don't be afraid to point your victories out to the devil. No victory is a small one. It takes winning the small battles to win the war. Be thankful for the small steps. That is the way you get to where you can make bigger steps.

Have positive expectancy. If you expect to fail, you will. You will be saying, "See, I never win." Even if by chance you happen to succeed, you'll say, "It will never happen again I was just lucky this time." You will achieve what you expect to achieve. Positive people always see obstacles as exciting challenges and opportunities.

Words can bless a person or curse them. They can heal or defeat you and those around you. How you see yourself and speak about yourself has a bearing on what your mind creates. Thoughts that are full of worry, doubt and fear will create that kind of life. We have what we have because we speak it into existence. How you speak about yourself has a direct bearing on what the mind creates.

Think and talk positive to yourself about your strengths and abilities. Stop thinking negative and always putting yourself down. I enjoy spending time with myself and building myself up by thinking and saying positive things about myself. During recovery, the person that has been in my corner the most saying things that made me determined to go on was me. I am my own best friend. I like being the positive encouraging person I am. Always building myself up with the faith and encouragement that my parents put in me long ago. "Thanks mom and dad."